GREAT BRITONS

NOVELISTS

Simon Adams

FRANKLIN WATTS
LONDON•SYDNEY

First published in 2007 by
Franklin Watts

Franklin Watts
338 Euston Road
London NW1 3BH

Franklin Watts Australia
Level 17/207 Kent Street
Sydney, NSW 2000

A CIP catalogue record for
this book is available from
the British Library.

Dewey number: 823.09

ISBN: 978 0 7496 7471 7

Printed in China

Franklin Watts is a division
of Hachette Children's
Books.

Designer: Thomas Keenes
Art Director: Jonathan Hair
Editor: Sarah Ridley
Editor-in-Chief:
John C. Miles
Picture Research:
Diana Morris

Picture credits:
Alinari/Topfoto: 41. Ashley
Cooper/Corbis: 45. Mary
Evans Picture Library: 7,
11, 16-17. John Hedgecoe/
Topfoto: 39. HIP/Topfoto:
9. Jeff Mitchell/Reuters/
Corbis: front cover, 42.
Picturepoint/ Topham: 12,
20, 23, 31, 35. Roger-
Viollet/Topfoto: 15, 36.
Ann Ronan Picture library/
HIP/Topfoto: 19, 26, 29.
Topfoto: 25. UPP/Topfoto:
32.

Every attempt has been made to
clear copyright. Should there be
any inadvertent omission please
apply to the publisher for
rectification.

CONTENTS

INTRODUCTION

Everyone who reads books has their favourite author or special novel, so trying to pick 24 novelists to represent the whole of British fiction is impossible. This book is therefore a representative selection that can be criticised, added to or altered as you, the reader, sees fit.

Most of the novelists included here have made a special contribution to the English novel, from Aphra Behn, the first woman writer and one of the first novelists, through Jane Austen and her observant novels on the society of the day, to Charles Dickens and his wonderful cast of characters. The 20th century is well represented by experimental novelists such as Virginia Woolf, and by such great storytellers as Graham Greene and D H Lawrence.

Writing novels has traditionally been a career open to women, unlike many other occupations, so 11 of our novelists are women. Also featured are writers of detective fiction (Arthur Conan Doyle), fantasy (Lewis Carroll), adventure (R L Stevenson) and political commentary (George Orwell). And no introduction to the English novel would be complete without J K Rowling, the most successful author of all time.

In recent years, British born or resident Black and Asian writers have made a huge contribution to English literature, yet few of them have yet established themselves as a major writer as they are mainly too young to have written many books. In future years, it should be possible to identify one or two that deserve inclusion here in their own right.

All the novelists featured in this book were born in Britain or have lived here for most of their lives. Excluded therefore are those novelists writing in English but who live in the USA, Canada, Ireland or elsewhere in the English-speaking world. The dates given after each novel are dates of publication, unless otherwise stated.

APHRA BEHN
THE FIRST ENGLISH PROFESSIONAL WOMAN WRITER

BORN Wye, near Canterbury, Kent, 10 July 1640
DIED London, 16 April 1689
AGE 48 years

Aphra Behn was not the first English novelist, and is by no means the best, but she is one of the most extraordinary. At a time when women did not have a profession, and many could barely read or write, she made her living as an author.

Aphra's father, Bartholomew Johnson, was a barber and her mother, Elizabeth, a nurse to the wealthy Culpepper family. Aphra grew up alongside their children, and in 1663–64 she probably visited the British colony of Suriname in South America with them. During this trip, she met an African slave leader, whose story she told in her novel, *Oroonoko*. Returning to England, Aphra married Johan Behn, a Dutch merchant, but the marriage did not last. However, she was soon employed by Charles II as a spy in the port of Antwerp during the Anglo-Dutch war of 1665–67. This work left her bankrupt

The English novel

The English novel we read today developed during the late 1600s, although the word itself is much older. From the early 1500s, the word 'novellae' and thus 'novel' described a short tale of love or adventure. Lengthier stories were described as 'romances' or 'histories'. The earliest full-length novels often took the form of a fictional autobiography or personal memoir (a 'memoir-novel', like *Oroonoko*) or a personal story told in the form of letters or a journal (an 'epistolary novel'). During the 1700s, novelists began to write through the voice of a third-person narrator, the most common form of the novel today. In 1824 Sir Walter Scott described the novel as 'a fictitious narrative ... accommodated to the ordinary train of human events'. That description is still useful today.

and she ended up in a debtor's prison. After her release in 1669, she paid off her debts by writing for a living.

Aphra Behn wrote 17 plays, many poems and four novels, the best of which is *Oroonoko: or, The Royal Slave: A True History*, written in 1688 and now considered to be one of the foundation stones of the English novel. It tells the story of Oroonoko, the heir to an African king, who falls in love with Imoinda. However, the king also loves her and in anger sells her into slavery. Oroonoko is captured by a European slaver and shipped off to Suriname, where he is reunited with Imoinda. He organises a slave revolt, but is betrayed by the local English governor and is executed. *Oroonoko* is remarkable as an early protest against the slave trade, which was not abolished in England until 1807, and because it honours and admires the African hero.

Aphra Behn was one of the first English novelists, and was one of the first women to make a living as a writer.

JONATHAN SWIFT
THE MASTER SATIRIST

BORN Dublin, Ireland,
30 November 1667
DIED Dublin,
19 October 1745
AGE 77 years

Although he was born and died in Dublin, Ireland, Jonathan Swift came from an English family and lived in Dublin at a time when Ireland was part of the United Kingdom. He wrote many books, of which *Gulliver's Travels* is the most famous.

After studying at Trinity College, Dublin, Swift became a vicar in the Protestant Church of Ireland. He was active in both religious and national politics and took a great interest in current affairs. However, because he was employed by the Church, he wrote all his works either under a made-up name (a pseudonym) or he put no name to it at all (anonymous).

Gulliver's Travels, originally published in 1726 as *Travels into Several Remote Nations of the World,* is a satire on human nature. Satire is a form of writing that pours scorn, or criticises, issues of the day through humour and ridicule.

The book, in four parts, tells the travel adventures of Lemuel Gulliver in his own words. The people of Lilliput are very small, the people of Brobdingnag very large, those in Laputa and elsewhere are devoted to music and maths but can't use them in any way, while the Houyhnhnms are horses ruling over

Daniel Defoe

Although written for adults, *Gulliver's Travels* is often read as a children's book. Another book with similar crossover appeal is *Robinson Crusoe*, which along with its sequel *Farther Adventures* was written by **DANIEL DEFOE** (1660–1731) in 1719. *Robinson Crusoe* is based on the true story of Alexander Selkirk, who lived on an uninhabited tropical island from 1704–09. Defoe adds many made-up incidents of his own, including a shipwreck, and keeps Robinson Crusoe on his island for 28 years. Because the book is so convincing and vivid, many people consider it to be the first great English novel.

Jonathan Swift led a dual life as a clergyman and a satirist, although for this he used a made-up name to hide his identity.

deformed humans called Yahoos. Swift makes the little people of Lilliput and their equally little neighbours across the sea look ridiculous, using their silly customs and feuds to poke fun at the court of King George I and at the constant warfare between England and France. Among his other satires, *A Modest Proposal* (1729) argues that the best way to end Ireland's poverty would be to fatten up all the underfed children and sell them to the rich landlords to eat, thus ending overpopulation and poverty at the same time. For these two and many other works, Swift is considered to be one of the best and funniest satirical writers.

HENRY FIELDING
CREATOR OF *TOM JONES*

BORN Sharpham Park, Somerset, 22 April 1707
DIED Lisbon, Portugal, 8 October 1754
AGE 47 years

Like many authors, Henry Fielding had another career to fall back on if his writing did not make him rich, in his case, the law. However, his literary works and indeed his private life often got him into trouble with the very law he was supposed to be upholding!

When he was 18, Fielding was involved in a drunken brawl in Lyme Regis in Dorset and was charged with assault. He then tried to abduct a beautiful, rich heiress and was again charged with assault. He quickly fled the town and went to London, where he started writing satirical plays for the theatre.

Some of his 25 plays were so critical of the government that parliament passed the Theatre Licensing Act of 1737. This law introduced the censorship of all plays by the Lord Chancellor and made it almost impossible to stage satirical plays.

Fielding therefore retired from the theatre, studied law and in 1740 became a barrister. He was appointed a Justice of the Peace for Westminster in 1748 and judged many cases from his court in Bow Street. In 1750 he set up the Bow Street Runners, a team of

The 18th century

The 18th century was a great time for English writing. **SAMUEL JOHNSON** (1709–84) compiled the first comprehensive dictionary of the English language (1755), defining more than 40,000 words. **JAMES BOSWELL** (1740–95) wrote Johnson's biography (1791), while both wrote journals of their joint tour of Scotland in 1773. **SAMUEL RICHARDSON** (1689–1761) wrote the melodramatic novel *Pamela* (1740–41), while **LAURENCE STERNE** (1713–68) wrote the nine-volume *Tristram Shandy* (1759–67), a hugely experimental work which has little narrative, no consistent plot and frequently wanders all over the place.

Henry Fielding, a novelist, a judge and the creator of today's police force.

agents who investigated crimes and arrested offenders on Fielding's orders. The Runners were London's first modern police force and the forerunner of today's Metropolitan Police.

While a successful lawyer, Fielding began to write novels. His first, *Shamela* (1741), parodied the recently published novel *Pamela*, by Samuel Richardson, while his second, *Joseph Andrews* (1742), dealt with Pamela's brother Joseph. Richardson was furious at these personal attacks and never forgave him. As if this controversy were not enough, Fielding attracted more when, in 1747, after the death of his first wife Charlotte, he married her maid Mary, who was already six months pregnant with their son.

Fielding's masterpiece is *Tom Jones* (1749), the hilarious story of how a foundling, an abandoned child, comes into a fortune. Tom is a rogue who lives by his wits, getting into so much trouble that he is eventually sentenced to death. In the end, his true parentage is discovered, he becomes the heir to a fortune, marries his sweetheart and promises to behave properly in the future.

Fielding described *Tom Jones* and his other novels as 'comic epics in prose'. He abandoned the epistolary style of Richardson and others, whose novels are written as letters, and wrote in the third person. Many people consider his books to be the first modern English novels.

JANE AUSTEN
AN ASTUTE AND HUMOROUS SOCIAL COMMENTATOR

BORN Steventon, Hampshire, 16 December 1775
DIED Winchester, Hampshire, 18 July 1817
AGE 41 years

Although only moderately successful in her own lifetime, Jane Austen is now considered to be one of the most important English novelists ever. Yet her entire work consists of just six novels, along with two unfinished novels and six pieces written when she was a teenager.

Jane Austen was the daughter of a clergyman, the seventh of eight children, and received a good education, which was unusual for girls at that time. Her life was not nearly as eventful as that of her main characters, for as an unmarried woman she remained socially and financially dependent on her parents. In 1801 she moved with her family to Bath, where she turned down an offer of marriage. When her father, George, died in 1805, she, her sister and their mother, both named Cassandra, moved to Southampton to live with her brother Frank.

Jane Austen is one of the most popular and well-respected writers in English fiction.

Mary Shelley

A very different kind of writer from Austen, **MARY SHELLEY** (1797–1851) was born into a highly political and literary family. Her father was William Godwin, a radical philosopher, while her mother was Mary Wollstonecraft, a feminist writer, who died giving birth to Mary. In 1814 she left England for Europe with Percy Bysshe Shelley, the poet, and married him in 1816. While in Switzerland, she wrote her most famous book, *Frankenstein* (1818), a horror story concerning a monster created by Frankenstein that turns upon its creator and eventually disappears to end its own life. The story is considered to be the first work of science fiction ever written and has been made into many film versions.

In 1809 they moved to a cottage on the estate of her wealthy brother Edward in Chawton, Hampshire. Here she spent the rest of her life, dying in 1817 probably of a disease often caused by tuberculosis.

Jane Austen published her six novels anonymously, a common practice by female authors at that time. The six – *Sense and Sensibility* (1811), *Pride and Prejudice* (1813), *Mansfield Park* (1814), *Emma* (1816), *Northanger Abbey* and *Persuasion*, both published after her death in 1818 – are all beautifully written stories that comment humorously on the society and manners of the day. All concern '3 or 4 families in a Country Village' (in Austen's words), or on a large estate. They focus on the unfortunate situation of well-bred, unmarried women, such as Austen herself, who through the customs of the day and the inheritance laws that favoured sons, were denied wealth and status in their own right.

Pride and Prejudice famously opens with the line: 'It is a truth, universally acknowledged, that a man in possession of a good fortune, must be in want of a wife.' The main characters are all young, single women and the rich young men whom they hope to marry. The women find love and happiness through moderation rather than romantic passion, which tends to end in disaster. Excessively practical or calculating behaviour also ends in the same way.

Jane Austen is best when she is describing women – she never wrote a scene involving just men, since she could never have witnessed such a meeting – and she is also excellent when, in Sir Walter Scott's words, she 'is describing the involvements of feelings and characters of ordinary life'. Although her books were written almost 200 years ago, they remain as fresh and as observant as when they first appeared.

CHARLES DICKENS
WORLD-FAMOUS NOVELIST AND SOCIAL CRITIC

BORN Portsmouth, Hampshire, 7 February 1812
DIED Higham, Kent, 9 June 1870
AGE 68 years

Charles Dickens is one of the best-loved and most popular English novelists of all time. During his lifetime he achieved massive popularity for his wonderful stories and memorable characters. All his books have remained in print to this day, as well as being turned into films, musicals, stage plays and television programmes.

Dickens was born the son of a naval pay clerk who moved first to Chatham, Kent and then to London. His early years were very happy and he read many books, but when he was 12 his father was imprisoned for debt. Charles then had to work 10 hours a day in a factory, pasting labels onto jars of boot polish, to earn enough money to pay for his lodgings and support his family. He used this experience of working life and harsh poverty in many of his books. His first book was *The Pickwick Papers* (1836–37), which, like most of his novels, originally appeared in monthly or weekly instalments in magazines and was then published as a complete book. *The Pickwick Papers* was a great success, and was quickly followed by *Oliver Twist* (1837–38), *Nicholas Nickleby* (1838–39)

The 19th-century storytellers

Dickens was not the only great storyteller of the 19th century. **SIR WALTER SCOTT** (1771–1832) wrote numerous historical novels, notably *Ivanhoe* (1819). **WILLIAM THACKERAY** (1811–63) is famous for *Vanity Fair* (1847–48), and other satirical and humorous novels about English society. **ANTHONY TROLLOPE** (1815–82) created two memorable series of books with interconnecting characters: the six 'Barsetshire' chronicles (1855–67), largely concerning the clergy, and the six 'Political' or 'Palliser' novels (1864–80), named after the main character, Plantagenet Palliser, and featuring his political life.

Charles Dickens was the creator of some of the most famous characters in English fiction.

and *The Old Curiosity Shop* (1840–41). Dickens went on to write 16 further novels. *A Christmas Carol* (1843) became one of the most famous Christmas stories of all time, and Dickens also wrote many other short stories, travel books and other works. He gave extensive public readings of his works, twice visiting the United States, where he was massively popular.

Most of Dickens's books are very long and written in a florid, descriptive style with a strong comic touch, although some people find them sensational or sentimental and his characters grotesque rather than life-like.

Many of his books, notably *David Copperfield* (1849–50), contain elements from his own life, while all make strong comments about the society of the day, criticising poverty and slum housing and attacking the poor running of the legal and financial systems.

THE BRONTË SISTERS
A FAMILY OF GREAT WRITERS

CHARLOTTE BRONTË
BORN Thornton,
  Yorkshire,
  21 April 1816
DIED Haworth,
  Yorkshire,
  31 March 1855
AGE 38 years

EMILY BRONTË
BORN Thornton,
  Yorkshire
  30 July 1818
DIED Haworth,
  Yorkshire,
  19 December 1848
AGE 30 years

ANNE BRONTË
BORN Thornton,
  Yorkshire,
  17 January 1820
DIED Scarborough,
  Yorkshire,
  28 May 1849
AGE 29 years

It is rare to find two great writers in the same family, but the Brontë sisters are unique in that all three are fine writers. During their lifetimes, their identities were largely a mystery, as their books were published under the names Currer (*Charlotte*), Ellis (*Emily*) and Acton (*Anne*) Bell. Today they are renowned for their direct and emotional novels.

The three Brontë sisters were the daughters of the Reverend Patrick Brontë and his wife, Maria, and were all born in Thornton, near Bradford in Yorkshire. Two older sisters both died young, from tuberculosis; their brother Bramwell (1817–48) had a brief life, too. In 1821, when Charlotte was five, the family moved a short distance to Haworth, where their father became the local clergyman. Sadly their mother died shortly afterwards and they were all cared for by her sister.

This 19th-century sketch depicts the three Brontë sisters with their brother, Bramwell.

They remained at Haworth for the rest of their lives, living in relative isolation on the Yorkshire moors, although both Charlotte and Emily spent a year in Brussels, Belgium.

Their first published book was a joint collection of poems, in May 1846, which sold very badly. All three then began their first novels. Charlotte wrote *The Professor*, which never found a publisher and only appeared in 1857, after her death, while Emily wrote *Wuthering Heights* and Anne wrote *Agnes Grey*. Both of these were published in 1847. Charlotte's second novel, *Jane Eyre*, appeared the same year, and she followed it up with two more novels *Shirley* (1849) and *Villette* (1853). Anne's second book, *The Tenant of Wildfell Hall*, appeared in 1848.

These seven books, plus the collection of poems, are the entire works of the Brontë sisters. Charlotte's books were considered coarse by the critics, while the innovatory structure of Emily's *Wuthering Heights* confused critics and got mixed reviews when it first appeared. Today, all three writers have been reassessed and their works are praised for their strong emotions and realistic feel. Their own tragic lives – all three died relatively young, from tuberculosis – have added to their appeal.

GEORGE ELIOT
A NOVELIST OF SOCIAL AND POLITICAL AWARENESS

BORN Nuneaton, Warwickshire, 22 November 1819
DIED Chelsea, London, 22 December 1880
AGE 61 years

Confusingly, George Eliot was not a man but a woman – Mary Anne Evans – who, like many other women writers of the period, used a male pseudonym to ensure that her works were taken seriously. Women did write under their own names at this time but their books were mainly romances. George Eliot was a much more serious novelist.

Mary Anne Evans was brought up in the Church of England but was influenced by non-conformist thinkers who challenged the established Church. She retained a strong religious belief in love and duty, and her books have many portraits of clergymen and religious dissenters. Indeed, many thought that George Eliot was a clergyman, or his wife. Her first books were translations of European religious writings, while her social conscience became evident when she worked as assistant editor of the campaigning, radical journal entitled the *Westminster Review*.

Mrs Gaskell

ELIZABETH GASKELL (1810–65) was the daughter of a clergyman who wrote her first novel, *Mary Barton*, in 1848 as a distraction from her sorrow at the death of her infant son. Five other novels followed, notably *Cranford* (1855), *North and South* (1855) and the unfinished *Wives and Daughters* (1866). She also wrote a celebrated biography of Charlotte Brontë in 1857 and many short novels and stories. Mrs Gaskell was very concerned with social issues and addressed the need for a better understanding between rich and poor, and between employers and workers. She is a great storyteller and carefully researched the background and details of her novels.

George Eliot, a serious novelist with a private life many considered scandalous at the time.

In 1851 she met the critic and philosopher George Henry Lewis and, although he was already married to someone else, in 1854 they set up home together. This relationship scandalised many people, but it made her very happy and gave her the support to begin writing novels.

George Eliot's first novel, *Adam Bede* (1859), was a great success, and was quickly followed by *The Mill on the Floss* (1860) and *Silas Marner* (1861). Four more novels followed, of which *Middlemarch* (1871–72) and *Daniel Deronda* (1874–76) are the best, as well as poems and other works. *Middlemarch* interweaves the stories of various friends and relatives in the town of Middlemarch on the eve of the crucial Reform Act of 1832. Her other novels are also politically and socially aware, and all feature well-rounded, believable people, which is why they are still so popular today.

LEWIS CARROLL
THE CREATOR OF ALICE

BORN Warrington,
Cheshire,
27 January 1832
DIED Guildford, Surrey,
14 January 1898
AGE 65 years

The creator of one of the most famous children's books of all time – *Alice's Adventures in Wonderland* – was not called Lewis Carroll at all. His real name was Charles Dodgson and he was a mathematician and skilled photographer.

Lewis Carroll. A boat trip with a girl gave him the inspiration for his most famous book.

Dodgson was educated at Rugby School and then Christ Church, Oxford, where he studied maths and became a maths lecturer in 1855. His family background was in the Church and he considered becoming an Anglican clergyman, but in 1862 he decided against it, for reasons that are still unknown. He did, however, become a very skilled photographer at a time when photography was still new, taking hundreds of photographs of children and adults, including such famous people as the scientist Michael Faraday and the poet Lord Tennyson.

In 1856 a new dean or head was appointed at Christ Church. Henry Liddell had a wife and four children, including a daughter, Alice. Dodgson grew fond of the family and often took the children on rowing trips. During one such expedition, on 4 July 1862, Dodgson told Alice a story that she loved. He later wrote down the story – then called *Alice's Adventures Under Ground* – and took it to a publisher, who printed it with illustrations by Sir John Tenniel in 1865 under the title *Alice's Adventures in Wonderland*. The book appeared under a pseudonym – Lewis Carroll – and was an instant success. A sequel, *Through the Looking Glass*, followed in 1871, to be followed by a long nonsense poem, *The Hunting of the Snark* (1876) and other works.

The success of the two Alice books lies in the fact that, unlike most children's books of the time, they had no moral and did not attempt to teach anything. Rather, they were great works of fantasy that continue to stimulate the interest and imagination of children of all ages, from 8 to 80.

Children's writing

The first books in Britain written specifically for children appeared during the 17th century, but all had a strong moral message. For entertainment, children read adult's books, such as **DANIEL DEFOE**'s *Robinson Crusoe* (1719). During the 19th century, the first collections of fairy stories appeared, notably those by the German **GRIMM** brothers (1823) and by the Danish **HANS** **CHRISTIAN ANDERSEN** (1846). Adventure stories, schoolboy tales, notably **THOMAS HUGHES**' *Tom Brown's Schooldays* (1857), family sagas and animal stories, such as **ANNA SEWELL**'s *Black Beauty* (1877), also became popular. So too did three great works of fantasy and imagination, **CHARLES KINGSLEY**'s *Water Babies* (1863) and the two books by **LEWIS CARROLL**.

THOMAS HARDY
THE NOVELIST AND POET OF WESSEX

BORN Higher Bockhampton, Dorset, 2 June 1840
DIED Dorchester, Dorset, 11 January 1928
AGE 87 years

Thomas Hardy started life as the son of a stonemason and builder, became an architect and then a successful novelist before giving that up to write poetry. By the end of his life, he had received many public honours and was buried in Westminster Abbey. Yet he was a gloomy and pessimistic man who found his fame hard to handle.

After attending school in Dorset, Hardy became apprenticed to an architect and in 1862 studied architecture in London. He returned to Dorset in 1867 and worked as an architect's assistant, winning prizes from the Royal Institute of British Architects and the Architectural Association. He began to write novels, but the first, *The Poor Man and the Lady*, written in 1867 remained unpublished and he destroyed the manuscript himself. Three more novels – including *Under the Greenwood Tree* (1872) – followed, and were published to mixed reviews. In 1874, the year he married his wife Emma, he published *Far From the Madding Crowd*, which was successful enough to allow him to give up architecture and write novels full time.

Over the next 25 years, Hardy produced 10 more novels, all of them set in the 'partly real, partly dream' county of Wessex, named after the Anglo-Saxon kingdom of southern England. Among the best are *The Return of the Native* (1876), *The Mayor of Casterbridge* (1886), *Tess of the d'Urbervilles* (1891) and *Jude the Obscure* (1895). He also wrote three collections of short stories. Almost all his books concern the struggle of people against fate and how they deal with great suffering and hardship. While many are also bleak, Hardy treats his rural characters affectionately and writes wonderfully about the natural world.

Both *Tess* and *Jude* were heavily criticised when they first appeared, some critics renaming *Jude* as 'Jude the Obscene'. Hardy therefore abandoned fiction, which he had always considered inferior, and turned to poetry. His first volume, *Wessex Poems*, a collection written over the course of 30 years, appeared in 1898 and was followed by seven more volumes. After he died, his *Collected Poems* (1930) was published, containing more than 900 poems, the best of which were written in 1912–13 in memory of his late wife. Although his poetry was not well received at the time, it is now much better thought of. His novels, however, have remained consistently popular.

Thomas Hardy, a novelist and poet whose fame brought him wealth but rarely happiness.

ROBERT LOUIS STEVENSON
BURIED TREASURE AND SPLIT PERSONALITIES

BORN Edinburgh,
Scotland,
13 November 1850
DIED Vailima, Samoa,
3 December 1894
AGE 44 years

Robert Louis Stevenson wrote some of the best-loved books of the 19th century, yet for years his work was criticised for being too popular and not serious or literary enough. Today, he is widely read around the world and his characters are among the best known in all fiction.

Stevenson was born into a long line of famous Scottish engineers and lighthouse builders. Unfortunately, he suffered from weak lungs and spent much of his childhood in bed. He studied engineering at Edinburgh University, but was not in the least bit interested in the subject and changed to read law, eventually qualifying as a barrister in 1875. But Stevenson never practised law, for he loved to travel and wanted to become a writer. Over the next few years, he travelled extensively around Europe and North America, writing about his canoe tour of Belgium and France in *An Inland Voyage* (1878) and his adventures with Modestine the donkey in *Travels with a Donkey in the Cevennes* (1879).

More travel pieces, short stories and essays appeared before his first novel

Adventure writers

Many other writers of the time wrote books of adventure and travel. **RUDYARD KIPLING** (1865–1936) set most of his stories in India, including his famous children's tales *The Jungle Book* (1894) and the *Just So Stories* (1902), while **RIDER HAGGARD** (1856–1925) set his two most famous books – *King Solomon's Mines* (1886) and *She* (1887) – in Africa. **JOSEPH CONRAD** (1857–1924) was a Russian-born Pole who only became a British subject in 1886 and spent many years at sea. Writing in what was his third language, Conrad set *Lord Jim* (1900) at sea, *Nostromo* (1904) in South America, and his most famous short story 'Heart of Darkness' (1902) in the jungles of Africa.

Stevenson ranged widely in his subject matter, from travel writing to Scottish history.

was published to great acclaim in 1883. *Treasure Island* is a story of seafarers, pirates and hidden treasure, and contains the memorable figure of the one-legged pirate, Long John Silver. Three years later, Stevenson published *The Strange Case of Dr Jekyll and Mr Hyde* (1886), a gripping and sinister tale about split personality. A trilogy of three historical novels set in Scotland – *Kidnapped* (1886), *The Master of Ballantrae* (1889) and *Kidnapped*'s sequel, *Catriona* (1893) – followed, as did many other novels, short stories and essays.

Stevenson's health was never good, and he left Europe for good in 1887, eventually settling on the tropical island of Upolu in Samoa, where he built a large house, called Vailima ('Five Rivers'). When he died, the islanders buried him on top of a cliff looking out across the Pacific Ocean.

ARTHUR CONAN DOYLE
CREATOR OF SHERLOCK HOLMES

BORN Edinburgh,
22 May 1859
DIED Crowborough,
Sussex, 7 July 1930
AGE 71 years

Sherlock Holmes is probably the most famous detective in the world, his considerable powers of logic and observation helping him solve many difficult crimes with his sidekick, Dr Watson. Holmes's creator was also a doctor, although not a very successful one.

Arthur Conan Doyle, the creator of one of the world's great detectives.

Conan Doyle qualified in medicine from Edinburgh University in 1881 and worked as a doctor first in Plymouth and then in Southsea, Portsmouth the following year. While he waited for patients to turn up, he began to write stories. His character, Sherlock Holmes, first appeared in the story 'A Study in Scarlet', published in *Beeton's Christmas Annual* of 1887. The story was then republished the following year as a full-length novel, illustrated by Conan Doyle's father, Charles. Also making its first appearance was Holmes' address of 221B Baker Street in London, which he shared with his landlady, Mrs Hudson, and with Dr Watson, who narrates this and most of the later stories.

In this first book, Holmes is depicted as a single-minded person with no interests apart from solving crimes. In later stories, he becomes a much more rounded character, with a huge knowledge of philosophy, music and beekeeping, among other subjects. In total, Holmes appeared in four novels and 56 stories, almost all appearing first as serials in *The Strand* monthly magazine.

Conan Doyle eventually tired of Holmes; he wanted to concentrate on writing historical novels. He decided to kill the detective off in 'The Adventure of the Final Problem' (1893), in which Holmes and his arch-enemy, Professor Moriarty, plunge to their death over a waterfall in Switzerland. His readers were appalled, so, in 1901 Conan Doyle brought Holmes back, setting *The Hound of the Baskervilles* (1901–02) in 1891, before his supposed death. This solution did not please everyone, and so Conan Doyle revived Holmes in 'The Adventure of the Empty House' (1894), set after his 'death', in 1894. Sherlock Holmes continues to fascinate his readers today.

Crime fiction

Crime fiction is the hugely popular genre of fiction that includes whodunits, mysteries and straightforward detective stories. **WILKIE COLLINS** (1824–89) wrote both the first mystery novel, *The Woman in White* (1859–60), and the first detective story, *The Moonstone* (1868). **ARTHUR CONAN DOYLE** did much to popularise the genre. Many of the best crime writers have been women, including **AGATHA CHRISTIE** (1890–1976), creator of Hercule Poirot and Mrs Marple, **DOROTHY L SAYERS** (1893–1957), creator of Lord Peter Wimsey, and, more recently **P D JAMES** (1920–), who features Commander Adam Dalgleish from Scotland Yard. Best of the modern writers is **IAN RANKIN** (1960–) and his Scottish detective John Rebus.

VIRGINIA WOOLF
A LITERARY AND FEMINIST INNOVATOR

BORN London,
25 January 1882
DIED Lewes, Sussex
28 March 1941
AGE 59 years

Artistic and literary life in Britain in the early 20th century was dominated by the Bloomsbury Group. They were a group of friends who originally met at the home of Vanessa and Virginia Stephen in Bloomsbury, an area of central London. Of all those associated with the group, Virginia Woolf, as she became, was its most important figure.

Virginia Stephen was born into a rich and artistic family – her father, Sir Leslie Stephen, was editor of the *Dictionary of National Biography* and was related to the novelist William Thackeray. In 1912 Virginia married Leonard Woolf, a novelist and social reformer. By then, she was writing her first novel, *The Voyage Out* (1915), the story of how a young woman discovers herself on a voyage. Seven more novels followed, notably *Mrs Dalloway* (1925), *To The Lighthouse* (1927) and *The Waves* (1931). Each one was increasingly experimental and innovatory: Woolf used 'stream-of-consciousness' writing, the written equivalent of a person's often jumbled thought processes, and explored the psychological as well as emotional motives of her characters.

The early 20th century

Two remarkable novelists were writing during the first half of the 20th century. A fellow member of the Bloomsbury Group, **E M FORSTER** (1879–1970) was preoccupied with English society and class differences in novels such as *A Room With A View* (1908), *Howards End* (1910) and *A Passage to India* (1924). **HENRY** **JAMES** (1843–1916), an American who lived for years in Britain and eventually became a British subject, examined the differences between the European and American characters in *The Wings of the Dove* (1902), *The Ambassadors* (1903) and *The Golden Bowl* (1904), among other novels.

Virginia Woolf, a literary innovator, feminist icon, and founder member of the influential Bloomsbury Group.

Woolf also wrote numerous short stories and non-fiction pieces, the most important of which was the extended essay 'A Room of One's Own' (1929). In it she describes the educational, social and financial disadvantages that women have faced throughout history, and argues that women would never write freely until they had their own room to write in and financial independence. For this and other works, Woolf is revered as a feminist writer, as well as a major literary innovator.

D H LAWRENCE
A MORAL BUT OFTEN CONTROVERSIAL WRITER

BORN Eastwood, Nottinghamshire, 11 September 1885
DIED Vence, France, 2 March 1930
AGE 44 years

Born David Herbert Lawrence, the son of a coal miner whose ex-schoolteacher mother was determined that her son should not become a miner, Lawrence was to become one of the most controversial novelists of his day. He studied to become a teacher and taught for two years but spent most of his life travelling and writing.

Lawrence published his first novel, *The White Peacock,* in 1911 but found fame with his third, *Sons and Lovers* (1913), a fairly autobiographical account of his early years. By now he had met Frieda Weekley, the German wife of his former professor in Nottingham and six years older than him. They eloped to Germany and spent their lives travelling, although they were always short of money and had a stormy relationship.

In 1915 Lawrence published his fourth novel *The Rainbow*, but it was seized by the police and declared obscene. Lawrence was always frank about sex and often used swear words in his writings; as a result, some people found his work offensive. Nine further novels followed, including *Women In Love* (1920) and *The Plumed Serpent* (1926), as well as numerous short stories, poems, travel writing and essays.

Towards the end of his life, Lawrence became seriously ill with tuberculosis. He and Frieda therefore went to the warm climate of Italy for his health and rented a villa near Florence. Here he wrote his most famous novel, *Lady Chatterley's Lover* (1928), the highly sexual story of an affair between a wealthy woman and her gamekeeper. The book was privately printed in Florence but did not appear in Britain until Penguin Books published the complete text in 1960. The company was then prosecuted under the Obscene Publications Act but was acquitted after a famous trial; the result had a huge impact on both literature and society during the 1960s and later, by redefining what was classed as acceptable.

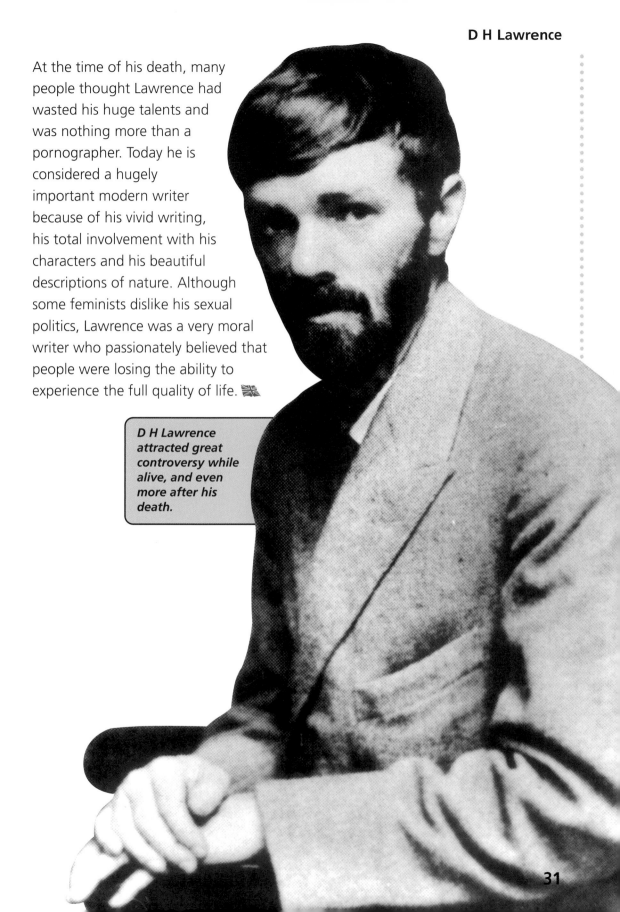

At the time of his death, many people thought Lawrence had wasted his huge talents and was nothing more than a pornographer. Today he is considered a hugely important modern writer because of his vivid writing, his total involvement with his characters and his beautiful descriptions of nature. Although some feminists dislike his sexual politics, Lawrence was a very moral writer who passionately believed that people were losing the ability to experience the full quality of life.

D H Lawrence attracted great controversy while alive, and even more after his death.

J R R TOLKIEN

CREATOR OF MIDDLE-EARTH, FATHER OF THE HOBBITS

BORN Bloemfontein, South Africa, 3 January 1892
DIED Oxford, England, 2 September 1973
AGE 81 years

To give him his full name and title, John Ronald Reuel Tolkien was Merton Professor of English Language and Literature at Oxford University from 1945–59 and a leading expert in Old and Middle English, the languages spoken in England from the 400s to about 1500. He is best known, however, as the author of *The Lord of the Rings*.

J R R Tolkien, the inventor of a much-loved fantasy world populated by hobbits and orcs.

Fantasy worlds

While at Oxford, Tolkien was a member of the Inklings, a loose group of friends with a similar interest in language and literature. One of its members was **C S LEWIS** (1898–1963), whose seven-volume *Chronicles of Narnia* (1950–56), starting with *The Lion, the Witch and the Wardrobe*, describe the adventures of a group of children in the magical world of Narnia. Another writer who invented an imaginary world was **MERVYN PEAKE** (1911–68), whose three-volume *Gormenghast* trilogy – *Titus Groan* (1946), *Gormenghast* (1950) and *Titus Alone* (1959) – tells the story of Titus, 77th Earl of Groan in his crumbling castle of Gormenghast.

Tolkien was born in South Africa, of British parents. His father's family originally came from Germany, hence his un-English surname. When Tolkien was only four, his father died and the family moved back to live in Birmingham, where his mother's family lived. Tolkien went to Oxford University to study first classics (ancient Greece and Rome) and then English language and literature. While at Oxford, Tolkien began to invent imaginary languages. He also came across the word 'middangeard' (meaning 'middle earth') in an Old English poem. With his imagination now stimulated, he began to write short stories concerning lost worlds populated by elves speaking strange languages, stories that formed the basis of *The Silmarillion* (1977) and *The Book of Lost Tales* (1983–84), both published after his death.

After military service in World War I, Tolkien eventually returned to Oxford as professor of Anglo-Saxon in 1925. He became a prominent academic, but continued to write and tell stories about his imaginary worlds. While marking an exam paper, he found that a student had left one page blank and had written on it: 'In a hole in the ground there lived a hobbit.' From this idea, he devised *The Hobbit*, published with great success in 1937. He came up with more stories, but the publishers rejected them as they wanted more Hobbit stories.

Tolkien set to work, eventually producing the three-volume *The Lord of the Rings: The Fellowship of the Ring*, *The Two Towers* (both 1954) and *The Return of the King* (1955). This vast work was an immediate success and gained mass appeal, becoming one of the cult books of the 1960s. Today, the trilogy has been filmed and is read around the world by people of all ages who love to follow the stories of Middle-earth, Gandalf and orcs, and how the hobbit Frodo Baggins takes a magical ring to the crack of doom. 🏴󠁧󠁢󠁿

GEORGE ORWELL
POLITICAL SATIRIST AND COMMENTATOR

BORN Motihari,
Bengal, India,
25 June 1903
DIED London,
21 January 1930
AGE 46 years

George Orwell was the pseudonym of Eric Blair, the son of a civil servant who worked in British India. He was born in India and won a scholarship to Eton, a top public school. Yet, despite this privileged upbringing, he became a free-thinking socialist and a leading social critic.

After he left Eton in 1921, Eric Blair returned to India and joined the Indian Imperial Police in Burma, an experience he used in his first novel *Burmese Days* (1934). This job turned him against the British Empire and he returned to England in 1927 determined to become a writer. He started to use the name George Orwell for his writings.

He had no money and did various jobs in London and Paris, an experience he wrote about in *Down and Out in Paris and London* (1933). Orwell then wrote two more novels, to mixed reviews, but his skills lay more as a reporter and essayist. *The Road to Wigan Pier* (1937) describes the poverty of working-class people in northern England during the

Political novelists

Apart from George Orwell, many other writers have dealt with political themes in their books. Two of the best are **ROBERT TRESSELL** (1870–1911), the pseudonym of Robert Noonan, a house painter and author of *The Ragged Trousered Philanthropists* (published after his death in 1914). The story concerns a group of working men in Mugsborough (based on Hastings) who are roused into political action

with a vision of a better society. The book deals with the greed and dishonesty of employers and workers alike and the social conditions that caused these vices. Another working-class novelist was **WALTER GREENWOOD** (1903–74), author of *Love on the Dole* (1933), a classic novel of life and love in a northern town during the great depression of the 1930s.

1930s. *Homage to Catalonia* (1938) is a highly critical account of the Spanish Civil War, in which he briefly fought and was seriously injured.

During World War II, Orwell worked on propaganda broadcasts for the BBC. By now, he was a respected social commentator, but he became world-famous for two novels published towards the end of his life. While in Spain, Orwell had become bitterly opposed to Russian communism under Stalin. *Animal Farm* (1945) is a political satire about the corruption of the Russian Revolution, while *Nineteen Eighty-Four* (1949) is a satire on Stalin's totalitarian government, a world in which 'Big Brother is watching you'. Today Orwell has entered the English language, as any form of government oppression or misleading political language is described as 'Orwellian'.

George Orwell, whose name has entered the English language and whose books are read worldwide.

GRAHAM GREENE
THE CHRONICLER OF GREENELAND

BORN Berkhamsted, Hertfordshire, 2 October 1904
DIED Vevey, Switzerland, 3 April 1991
AGE 86 years

Many writers describe imaginary worlds in their books, but not many have an entire world named after them. Graham Greene was the exception, a novelist whose characters often inhabit the sleazy world of Greeneland.

Greene wrote 26 novels as well as three travel books, four short story collections, four autobiographies, eight plays and 21 screenplays. His books were taken seriously, as well as being hugely popular, with many of his novels, notably *Brighton Rock* (1938) and *The Third Man* (1949), being made into successful films. A devout Roman Catholic, he objected strongly to being described as a Catholic novelist, preferring the description of a 'novelist who happened to be Catholic'. Yet Catholic religious themes are at the heart of many of his earlier books, notably *The Power and the Glory* (1940), the story of a

The prolific Graham Greene, whose characters are often troubled by doubt or despair.

20th-century novelists

The 20th century has been a glorious time for the British novel, with many writers producing books of outstanding quality. **EVELYN WAUGH** (1903–66) wrote novels of social comedy and satire, including *Vile Bodies* (1930), set in Mayfair, *Scoop* (1938), the hilarious story of a nature writer mistakenly sent by a newspaper to cover a war, and *Brideshead Revisited* (1945), a more serious book about an aristocratic Catholic family in decline that was made into a very successful television series in 1980. **ANTHONY POWELL** (1905–2000) wrote the 12-volume sequence of novels called *A Dance to the Music of Time* (1951–75), setting a huge cast of characters against modern British history. **IRIS MURDOCH** (1919–99) was once a lecturer in philosophy and her novels are often about morals or the struggle between good and evil. **MURIEL SPARK** (1918–2006) wrote short, elegant and sometimes eccentric novels, the most famous of which is *The Prime of Miss Jean Brodie* (1961), the portrait of an Edinburgh schoolmistress and her favoured pupils, her 'crème de la crème'.

self-destructive priest in Mexico at a time when its government was repressing organised religion.

Greene was born into a rich family, his father the headmaster of Berkhamsted School. Greene attended the school as a boarder but was extremely unhappy and, by his own account, tried to commit suicide several times. He received treatment for depression and went on to Oxford University, where he published an unsuccessful book of poetry. From 1926–30 he worked as a subeditor on the *Times* newspaper. His first novel *The Man Within* (1929) was a success, so he left the newspaper to become a full-time writer. His next two novels were failures, and he later disowned them, but *Stamboul Train* (1932) was well received and was followed by many more books.

Greene travelled extensively throughout his life, using his experiences as the basis for his work. Many of his novels are set in poor parts of the world – West Africa, Vietnam, Haiti, Mexico – and many of them feature characters troubled by doubt or despair. He was also intrigued by the world of espionage and international politics, as he had been recruited into the MI6 secret service during the 1930s and submitted reports to British intelligence throughout his life. Whatever the subject matter, all his books are distinguished by a lean and realistic style of writing that is immediately recognisable.

WILLIAM GOLDING
NOBEL AND BOOKER PRIZE WINNER

BORN St Columb
Minor, Cornwall,
19 September 1911
DIED near Truro,
Cornwall,
19 June 1993
AGE 81 years

William Golding's reputation rests on a handful of books, yet such was their power and moral force that he was awarded the Nobel Prize for Literature in 1983, one of only seven Britons to have won it in its 105-year history.

Golding came from a political family: his father was a schoolmaster with radical beliefs, his mother a strong supporter of a women's right to vote. He studied natural sciences and English language at Oxford University and then taught English at a school in Salisbury.

During World War II, he fought in the Royal Navy and took part in the D-Day landings in Normandy in June 1944. After the war, he returned to teaching, only giving it up in 1961 when his books had become successful. His first novel, *Lord of the Flies* (1954), was an

British Noble Prize winners

The annual Nobel Prize for Literature is the greatest literary prize in the world. The prize, first awarded in 1901, is funded from the fortune left by Alfred Nobel, the Swedish inventor of dynamite, and goes to 'the person who shall have produced in the field of literature the most outstanding work of an idealistic tendency'. **WILLIAM GOLDING** is not the only British winner: **RUDYARD KIPLING** (1865-1936) won it in 1907, **JOHN GALSWORTHY** (1867-1933) in 1932, the poet **T S ELIOT** (1888-1965) in 1948, the philosopher and peace campaigner **BERTRAND RUSSELL** (1872-1970) in 1950, and the playwright and poet **HAROLD PINTER** (1930-) in 2005. Most surprising winner was **WINSTON CHURCHILL**, the British prime minister who was awarded the prize in 1953 for his history writing, particularly his books about the two world wars and the English-speaking peoples. Many people felt that he was awarded the prize to honour him, not his writings, as the only other prize available, for peace, would have been inappropriate for a wartime leader.

immediate success and has twice been filmed. It tells of a group of schoolchildren who crash land on a desert island. Their lives descend into savagery until the arrival of a rescue officer. *The Inheritors* (1955), his second novel, is equally brutal, telling how human ancestors killed off their more gentle relatives in order to survive. In *Pincher Martin* (1956) and *Free Fall* (1959), Golding explores the main problems of life, such as survival and human freedom. Although there is no single theme to unite these and later novels, Golding deals principally with evil and often presents isolated individuals or small groups in extreme situations struggling to exist.

In all, Golding wrote 14 novels, as well as a book of poems and two books of essays. His later books did not earn the praise of his earlier work, although towards the end of his life he wrote *To the Ends of the Earth*, a remarkably vivid historical trilogy about the sea consisting of *Rites of Passage* (1980), *Close Quarters* (1987) and *Fire Down Below* (1989). *Rites of Passage* earned him the prestigious Booker Prize in 1980 for the best novel published that year. His other claim to fame, apart from his books, is that he suggested to his neighbour James Lovelock that his revolutionary theory that the Earth is a self-sustaining organism should be named Gaia, after the Greek earth goddess.

William Golding, the much-respected novelist and Nobel Prize Winner.

IAN McEWAN
A GRIPPING, SOMETIMES SINISTER WRITER

BORN Aldershot, England, 21 June 1948

Of all the novelists writing today, Ian McEwan is one of the most interesting and most controversial. He is never afraid to tackle big emotional issues, such as child abduction, and he uses human psychology and illness as themes for his books. Some of his books are very unsettling, once earning him the nickname 'Ian Macabre'.

McEwan was educated at the universities of Sussex and East Anglia. His first two books – *First Love, Last Rites* (1975) and *In Between The Sheets* (1978) – were both collections of sinister but also darkly humorous short stories. *The Cement Garden* (1978), his first novel, tells the story of four children who have been suddenly orphaned and must now look after themselves in their house. *The Child in Time* (1987) again concentrates on childhood, this time from the view of the parents whose baby daughter is abducted. From then on, his books become weightier in both length and, if possible, content. *Black*

Modern British writers

Alongside Ian McEwan are a number of writers who have achieved great success in recent years. Although born in Japan, **KAZUO ISHIGURO** (1954–) was brought up in England. *An Artist of the Floating World* (1982) deals with his home town of Nagasaki after the detonation of the atomic bomb over the city, while *The Remains of the Day* (1989) is set in the country house of an English lord in the years before World War II. **MARTIN AMIS** (1949–) is a very inventive writer with a great command of the English language, as shown in books such as *Money* (1984), *London Fields* (1989) and *Time's Arrow* (1991), in which time runs backwards throughout the entire book. **ANGELA CARTER** (1940–92) updated fairy stories to bring out their dark, sinister qualities: her best novel, *Nights At The Circus* (1984) concerns a Victorian circus performer who really can fly.

Dogs (1992) is a parable of evil in which an English couple have an encounter with two terrifying dogs. Many people consider his next novel, *Enduring Love* (1997), to be his best, a story of a stranger's obsessive love for a man that drives that man to the edge of madness.

In 1998 McEwan won the Booker Prize for his novel, *Amsterdam*. He then followed this up with *Atonement* (2001), an extraordinary story of how one young girl's imagination causes an innocent man to be imprisoned, an act for which she must atone, or make amends, for the rest of her life. His latest novel, *Saturday* (2005), tells of a day in the life of Henry Perowne, a neurosurgeon, and a patient suffering from an incurable disease. Like all his books, it is extraordinarily powerful in its content and emotional impact.

Ian McEwan, a master storyteller who tackles big emotional issues in an often unsettling way.

J K ROWLING
CREATOR OF HARRY POTTER

BORN Yate, South Gloucestershire, 31 July 1965

Of all the famous novelists mentioned in this book, J K Rowling has been read by far the largest number of people. She has written only a handful of books, and they are all for children, yet they have made her the richest, most successful writer in history.

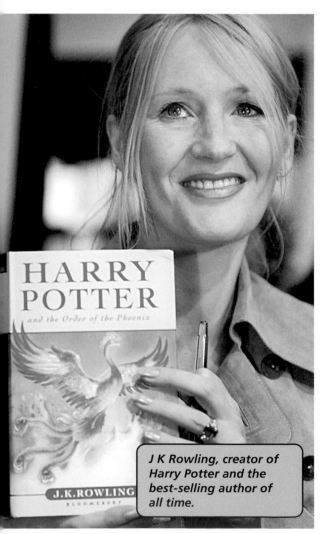

J K Rowling, creator of Harry Potter and the best-selling author of all time.

J K Rowling studied French and Classics at Exeter University and for a time taught English as a foreign language in Portugal, where her daughter was born in 1992. In 1994 she moved to Edinburgh with her baby daughter and wrote much of her first book – *Harry Potter and the Philosopher's Stone* – in local cafés whenever her daughter had fallen asleep. The book was the first in a series of seven books about a young wizard and his adventures at Hogwarts School of Witchcraft and Wizardry. Twelve publishers refused the book before Bloomsbury publishers accepted it after the chairman's eight-year-old daughter, Alice, read the first chapter and demanded to read more. Before the book was published in 1997, the author was asked to write under two initials, rather than use her first name, as the publishers felt that young boys would not read a book written by a woman. The 'K' is her grandmother Kathleen's

Children's literature

Children's books have become increasingly interesting and well written in recent years. **ROALD DAHL** (1916–90) has created some hugely popular books, including *James and the Giant Peach* (1961) and *Charles and the Chocolate Factory* (1964); his stories are told from a child's point of view and contain a lot of black humour and sometimes violence. **JACQUELINE WILSON** (1945–) writes stories for children about modern British children facing problems in their lives, such as divorce, loss, homelessness or abuse; in 2005 she became the Children's Laureate, the official champion of children's books and reading. Like J K Rowling, **PHILIP PULLMAN** (1946–) writes for children but adults read his books too, particularly his trilogy of fantasy novels: *His Dark Materials: Northern Lights* (1995), *The Subtle Knife* (1997) and *The Amber Spyglass* (2000).

name, as Joanne has no middle name herself. She was also advised to get a day job, as books for children do not sell that well!

All that changed when the book started to win literary prizes and became a massive success in the USA. Five more books in the series – one for each of Harry's school years – have now been published: *Harry Potter and the Chamber of Secrets* (1998), *Harry Potter and the Prisoner of Azkaban* (1999), *Harry Potter and the Goblet of Fire* (2000), *Harry Potter and the Order of the Phoenix* (2003) and *Harry Potter and the Half-Blood Prince* (2005). The seventh and final book in the series is *Harry Potter and the Deathly Hallows* (2007).

The books have become a worldwide phenomenon, selling hundreds of millions of copies to both children and adults. To spare adults the embarrassment of reading a children's book, their edition has a different cover. Many people who buy the books say they have never read another book in their lives before they read their first Harry Potter story. The series has also reached a vast audience at the cinema.

Joanne Rowling has also written two spin-offs from the series: *Fantastic Beasts and Where to Find Them* (2001) was written to benefit the Comic Relief charity, while *Quidditch Through the Ages* (2001) is the history of the airborne ballgame played on broomsticks by Harry and his schoolmates.

It will be fascinating to see what Rowling writes after the *Harry Potter* series ends. She has said that she will not continue the stories, but like George Lucas and *Star Wars*, will she be tempted to produce a prequel or two? We will have to wait and see!

BRITISH BLACK AND ASIAN WRITERS
A NEW GENERATION OF WRITERS

In recent years, a number of young Black or Asian writers born or resident in Britain and writing in English have begun to attract attention for their work. With the exception of Caryl Phillips and Salman Rushdie, none of them have yet fully established themselves, as they have written too few books. There is no doubt, however, that in future years, Black and Asian writers will play a substantial part in the development of the English novel.

Andrea Levy (1956–) was born in London to Jamaican parents: all four of her novels explore from different viewpoints the problems faced by black British-born children of Jamaican immigrants. Her most recent, prize-winning novel, *Small Island* (2004), explores the interaction between a Jamaican recruit to the Royal Air Force, who comes to live in Britain with his wife in 1948, and their white landlady and her recently demobbed husband.

Caryl Phillips (1958–) was born on the West Indian island of St Kitts but brought up in Yorkshire. His eight novels all deal with aspects of race: *Crossing the River* (1993) looks back to slavery; *A Distant Shore* (2003) addresses racial differences today.

Monica Ali (1967–) was born in Bangladesh but moved with her family to Britain when she was three. Like Zadie Smith (below), Ali writes about race and community in Britain: her novel, *Brick Lane* (2003), is set in the heart of London's Bangladeshi community and follows the life of Nazneen, a young Bangladeshi who comes to London to marry a much older man.

Zadie Smith (1975–) was born in London to a Jamaican mother and an English father. Her three novels all focus on people's different lives, religions and race. *White Teeth* (2000) is built around three families, one British and Jamaican, one Bangladeshi and one Jewish and Catholic; *The Autograph Man* (2002) features a Jewish/Chinese character, while *On Beauty* (2005) follows the lives of a black British family living in the USA.

Unlike the other novelists discussed here, **Salman Rushdie** (1947–) is more concerned with wider historical and social issues, particularly about the Indian subcontinent. Rushdie was born and brought up in India and then moved to Pakistan at the age of 14. He was educated in England and worked in advertising in London before becoming a full-time writer. His second novel, *Midnight's Children* (1981), was a huge success, winning that year's Booker Prize and the 'Booker of Bookers' in 1993 for the best novel awarded the Booker in its first 25 years. The novel loosely follows the history of India before and after independence through the story of Saleem Sinai, born at the exact moment India became independent. Like many of his books, it is written in a magic realist style, in which magical elements appear in an otherwise realistic setting.

In February 1989 Rushdie's life was turned upside down. Ayatollah Khomeini, leader of Iran, issued a *fatwa* or legal judgement against Rushdie requiring his execution because his novel *The Satanic Verses* (1988) was judged to be 'blasphemous against Islam'. A bounty was offered for his death, his book was publicly burned and bookshops firebombed. Rushdie went into hiding until 1998, when Iran publicly said that it would do nothing to harm Rushdie, although it would not lift the fatwa itself.

Rushdie continues to hold strong views. His novels, up to and including his latest book, *Shalimar the Clown* (2005), have influenced a generation of Indian writers both in the subcontinent and in Britain.

Brick Lane, London, the setting for Monica Ali's best-selling 2003 novel. It is the heart of London's Bangladeshi community.

Glossary

Anonymous A writer whose name is unknown or deliberately withheld.

Autobiography An account of a person's life written by that person.

Biography An account of a person's life written by someone else.

Bloomsbury Group A group of writers, artists, economists and others in the early years of the 20th century who reacted against the social and artistic restrictions of the Victorian era and supported avant-garde or experimental art and literature.

Booker Prize Literary prize awarded annually since 1969 for the best original full-length novel written by a British, Commonwealth or Irish citizen in the English language; originally and officially called the Booker-McConnell Prize after the company that sponsored it, in 2002 it was renamed the Man Booker Prize after the Man Group investment company that now sponsors it.

Crime fiction A novel that deals with crimes, criminals and their motives, and their detection by police detectives or amateur sleuths.

Dissenter Someone who refuses to conform with organised religion.

Epic A lengthy novel or poem which has heroic deeds as its main subject.

Epistolary Written in the form of letters or diary entries.

Fiction An invented story that is not true or real.

Genre A category or type of literature, such as science or crime fiction.

Historical novel A novel with an historical background or main character(s).

Journal A record of events kept on a regular basis in a book, such as a diary.

Magic realism A literary style in which magical elements appear in an otherwise realistic setting.

Melodrama A novel or play with overdramatic emotion and behaviour.

Memoir A biography or historical account of events.

Narrative account Report or story of events or experiences.

Non-conformist Someone who refuses to conform to or dissents from organised religion.

Novel An extended piece of prose writing that is totally or largely fictitious.

Novella A short novel.

Parable A story that uses familiar events to tell a moral or religious message.

Parody A novel or poem that mimics or makes fun out of the style of another author or a type of writing in a humorous or satirical way.

Poetry Literature written in rhyme or verse.

Pornographer Person who writes, draws or films material designed to stimulate sexual excitement.

Propaganda The organised distribution of information or a particular set of ideas, designed to persuade people to think or act in a particular way.

Prose Spoken or written language.

Pseudonym A made-up name used by an author to disguise his or her identity.

Satire A novel, play or poem in which issues of the day are held up to scorn by means of ridicule.

Science fiction The literary genre that makes imaginative use of scientific knowledge or ideas, often set in the future.

Sequel A novel that continues a previously published story.

Story The narration (telling) of a series of fictional events.

Third person Pronouns such as he, she, it, or they, referring to objects or individuals that are not the speaker (the first person) or the person spoken to (the second person); a third-person narrative is one written by a narrator who is not part of the story and stands outside it.

Tuberculosis Infectious disease, commonly called TB, caused by a bacterium and which frequently affects the lungs.

Whodunnit ('Who done it?') A complex, plot-driven detective story in which clues are scattered throughout the book, allowing the reader to discover who committed the crime before it is revealed in the final pages.

Some useful websites

http://en.wikipedia.org/wiki/Main_Page
Wikipedia's biographies of everyone mentioned in this book.

http://en.wikipedia.org/wiki/First_novel_in_English
Wikipedia's entry on the first novel in English.

http://www.bbc.co.uk/history/historic_figures/
BBC website giving brief biographies.

http://www.tolkiensociety.org/tolkien/org/
The official site of the Tolkien Society.

http://www.jkrowling.com
The official site of J K Rowling.

SOME PLACES TO VISIT

Westminster Abbey, London
The burial site of many of Britain's best authors and playwrights, as well as its kings and queens.

Chawton, Hampshire
Jane Austen's cottage, now a museum.

Charles Dickens Birthplace Museum, Portsmouth
The house where Dickens was born, furnished in the style of the time with items associated with Dickens and his life.

Brontë Parsonage Museum, Haworth, Yorkshire
Home of the Brontës from 1820 to 1861.

Charleston Farmhouse, near Lewes, East Sussex
The extraordinarily decorated country home of the Bloomsbury Group.

King's Cross Station, London
See if you can find Platform 9 $\frac{3}{4}$, from where Harry Potter first set out to Hogwarts School.

The British Library, London
The largest reference and research library in Britain, with a copy of almost every book ever published in the UK.

Index

These are the lists of contents for each title in *Great Britons*:

LEADERS
Boudica • Alfred the Great • Richard I • Edward I • Robert Bruce
Owain Glyndwr • Henry V • Henry VIII • Elizabeth I
Oliver Cromwell • The Duke of Marlborough • Robert Walpole
Horatio Nelson • Queen Victoria • Benjamin Disraeli
William Gladstone • David Lloyd George • Winston Churchill
Clement Attlee • Margaret Thatcher

CAMPAIGNERS FOR CHANGE
John Wycliffe • John Lilburne • Thomas Paine • Mary Wollstonecraft
William Wilberforce • Elizabeth Fry • William Lovett
Edwin Chadwick • Lord Shaftesbury • Florence Nightingale
Josephine Butler • Annie Besant • James Keir Hardie • Emmeline Pankhurst
Eleanor Rathbone • Ellen Wilkinson • Lord David Pitt • Bruce Kent
Jonathon Porritt • Shami Chakrabati

NOVELISTS
Aphra Behn • Jonathan Swift • Henry Fielding • Jane Austen
Charles Dickens • The Brontë Sisters • George Eliot • Lewis Carroll
Thomas Hardy • Robert Louis Stevenson • Arthur Conan Doyle
Virginia Woolf • D H Lawrence • J R R Tolkien • George Orwell
Graham Greene • William Golding • Ian McEwan • J K Rowling
Caryl Phillips • Andrea Levy • Zadie Smith
Monica Ali • Salman Rushdie

ARTISTS
Nicholas Hilliard • James Thornhill • William Hogarth
Joshua Reynolds • George Stubbs • William Blake • J M W Turner
John Constable • David Wilkie • Dante Gabriel Rossetti
Walter Sickert • Gwen John • Wyndham Lewis • Vanessa Bell
Henry Moore • Barbara Hepworth • Francis Bacon • David Hockney
Anish Kapoor • Damien Hirst

ENGINEERS
Robert Hooke • Abraham Darby • James Watt • John MacAdam
Thomas Telford • George Cayley • George Stephenson • Robert Stephenson
Joseph Paxton • Isambard Kingdom Brunel • Henry Bessemer
Joseph Bazalgette • Joseph Whitworth • Charles Parsons • Henry Royce
Nigel Gresley • Lord Nuffield • Harry Ricardo • Frank Whittle • Norman Foster

SCIENTISTS
John Dee • Robert Boyle • Isaac Newton • Edmond Halley • William Herschel
Michael Faraday • Charles Babbage • Mary Anning • Charles Darwin
Lord Kelvin • James Clerk Maxwell • Ernest Rutherford • Joseph Rotblat
Dorothy Hodgkin • Alan Turing • Francis Crick • Stephen Hawking
John Sulston • Jocelyn Bell Burnell • Susan Greenfield

SPORTING HEROES
WG Grace • Arthur Wharton • Kitty Godfree • Roger Bannister
Stirling Moss • Jackie Stewart • Bobby Moore • George Best
Gareth Edwards • Barry Sheene • Ian Botham • Nick Faldo
Torville and Dean • Lennox Lewis • Daley Thompson • Steve Redgrave
Tanni Grey-Thompson • Kelly Holmes • David Beckham • Ellen McArthur

MUSICIANS
William Byrd • Henry Purcell • George Frideric Handel • Arthur Sullivan
Edward Elgar • Henry Wood • Ralph Vaughan Williams • Noel Coward
Michael Tippet • Benjamin Britten • Vera Lynn
John Dankworth and Cleo Laine • Jacqueline Du Pre
Eric Clapton • Andrew Lloyd Webber • Elvis Costello
Simon Rattle • The Beatles • Courtney Pine • Evelyn Glennie